Campbell's

No-Time-To-Cook RECIPES

PUBLICATIONS INTERNATIONAL, LTD.

This edition was produced by the Global Publishing division of Campbell Soup Company, Campbell Place, Camden, NJ 08103-1799.

Senior Managing Editor:	Pat Teberg
Assistant Editors:	Peg Romano, Joanne Fullan
Senior Marketing Manager:	Brent Walker
Public Relations Manager:	Mary Beth Kramer
Marketing Research Manager:	Holly McGrath
Global Consumer Food Center:	Jane Freiman, Nancy Speth
Photography:	Peter Walters Photography/Chicago
Photographers:	Peter Walters, Peter Ross
Photo Stylist/Production:	Betty Karslake
Food Stylists:	Teri Ernst, Lois Hlavac, Carol Parik
Assistant Food Stylist:	Moisette Sintov McNerney

This edition published by Publications International, Ltd., 7373 N. Cicero Ave., Lincolnwood, IL 60646.

Pictured on the front cover *(clockwise from top left):* Chicken-Broccoli au Gratin *(page 14)*, Savory Pork and Vegetables *(page 62)* and Glazed Vegetables *(page 72)*.

Pictured on the back cover *(clockwise from top right):* Vegetable Rotini *(page 78)*, Lemon Asparagus Chicken *(page 18)* and Skillet Mac 'n' Beef *(page 54)*.

ISBN: 0-7853-1803-8

Manufactured in the U.S.A.

8 7 6 5 4 3 2 1

Preparation and Cooking Times: Each of these recipes was developed and tested in Campbell's Global Consumer Food Center by professional home economists. Use "Prep Time" and "Cook Time" given with each recipe as guides. The preparation times are based on the approximate amount of time required to assemble the recipe *before* baking or cooking. These times include preparation steps, such as chopping; mixing; cooking rice, pasta, vegetables; etc. The fact that some preparation steps can be done simultaneously or during cooking is taken into account. The cook times are based on the minimum amount of time required to cook, bake or broil the food in the recipes.

For sending us glassware, flatware, dinnerware and serving dishes used in recipe photographs, a special thanks to: *Dansk International Designs Ltd.*, Mount Kisco, NY, on pages 65, 69, 75 and 91; *Gorham Inc.*, Providence, RI, on pages 13, 29, 33, 37, 41, 43, 63, 67 and 81; and *Oneida Ltd.*, Oneida, NY, on pages 11, 17, 19, 23, 49, 73, 83 and 85.

For sending us kitchen equipment used in recipe technique photos, a special thanks to: *Corning Incorporated*, Corning, NY; *Ekco Housewares, Inc.*, Franklin Park, IL; and *Regal Ware, Inc.*, Kewaskum, WI, on pages 10, 22, 30, 38, 46, 52, 60, 66, 72, 78 and 82.

No-Time-To-Cook
RECIPES

M'm! M'm! Good! Cooking Begins with Campbell's Soups

Campbell has taken the frazzle out of mealtime and put the sizzle back in! With Campbell's new cookbook, *No-Time-To-Cook Recipes,* you're just pages away from enjoying over 50 great-tasting, easy-to-prepare recipes using America's favorite cooking ingredient: Campbell's Soup.

Here, you'll find delicious recipes guaranteed to speed your way to serving the best recipes ever—in 45 minutes or less. Better yet, most can be made from start to finish in less than 30 minutes!

Cooking with flavorful Campbell's Soup saves you valuable kitchen time because it eliminates the need for extra ingredients *and* helps you streamline preparation steps. We've included dozens of tasty recipes perfect for today's busy schedules. And every recipe is beautifully photographed so you'll know what it looks like *before* you begin cooking.

So for delicious recipes that take practically *no time to cook,* turn the page and get ready, set... go! From our Kitchens to yours, we give you these Campbell favorites—they're *M'm! M'm! Good!*

Campbell's Family of Cooking Soups

NO-TIME-TO-COOK KITCHEN TIPS

When there's *no time to cook,* here are some helpful suggestions on how to get in and out of the kitchen—*fast!*

ORGANIZING YOUR KITCHEN

- Keep utensils needed for each work area (countertop, sink and range) within easy reach.
- Keep countertops free from clutter.
- Alphabetize herbs and spices.
- Turn labels on cans or boxes toward the front of your shelves so you can read them at a glance.
- Keep food processor and other time-saving appliances within easy reach.
- Store frequently used items in the same place, so there's no need to spend time hunting for them.

PLANNING AHEAD

- Plan a week of menus turning *leftovers* into *"planned overs."* For example, serve roast chicken for a weekend dinner and use the *planned over* cooked chicken to make Chicken Quesadillas (page 38) for Tuesday's dinner.
- Keep a grocery list on the refrigerator door or other convenient location to jot down items as they are used up.
- Do as much of the grocery shopping as possible at one time and avoid supermarket *rush hours*—times when the checkout lines are long and the aisles are crowded.
- Purchase time- and work-saving ingredients. For example, although preshredded cheese, supermarket salad-bar makings and skinless, boneless chicken breasts may cost a few pennies more, often they are well worth the extra money spent. Items like these will reduce valuable time spent in the kitchen.
- When cooking pasta or rice for dinner, cook a double batch to use in another meal or recipe, such as Beef and Mozzarella Bake (page 50).
- Plan easy-to-make, fast-to-fix entrées such as Lemon Asparagus Chicken (page 18) or Skillet Broccoli Chicken (page 36). Both can be made in only 25 minutes!

PREPARING AND COOKING MEALS

- Before you begin, organize the preparation of the meal.
- When using a recipe, read it first so you'll be familiar with the ingredients and cooking method.
- Plan to overlap preparation and cooking steps. For example, while the Chili con Carne simmers (page 56), assemble the salad and set the table. Or, while waiting for water to boil or meat to brown, start chopping vegetables, opening cans or mixing a filling.
- Assemble all ingredients *before* you begin cooking.
- Begin meal preparation by starting with the food that takes the longest to cook. Start heating the water to cook rice or noodles *first,* before browning meat, chopping vegetables, opening cans or measuring ingredients.
- Clean up as you cook.
- Make mealtime *family time* and involve the whole family. Divide the meal preparation into parts, giving each member a job to do. For example, a young child can set the table while an older child makes the salad.

Simply Delicious Poultry

BROCCOLI–CHEESE CHICKEN

For an easy garnish, sprinkle with toasted sliced almonds before serving.

1 tablespoon margarine *or* butter
4 skinless, boneless chicken breast halves (about 1 pound)
1 can (10¾ ounces) CAMPBELL'S condensed Broccoli Cheese Soup
2 cups fresh broccoli flowerets
⅓ cup water *or* milk
⅛ teaspoon black pepper
Fresh oregano sprigs *and* fresh kumquats or orange slices for garnish

■ In 10-inch skillet over medium-high heat, in hot margarine, cook chicken 10 minutes or until browned on both sides. Remove; set aside.

■ In same skillet, combine soup, broccoli, water and black pepper. Heat to boiling. Return chicken to skillet. Reduce heat to low. Cover; cook 10 minutes or until chicken is no longer pink and broccoli is tender, stirring occasionally. Garnish with oregano and kumquats, if desired.

Makes 4 servings	**Prep Time: 10 minutes** **Cook Time: 25 minutes**

Asparagus-Cheese Chicken: Prepare Broccoli-Cheese Chicken as directed above, *except* substitute 12 fresh *asparagus spears,* cut into 2-inch pieces, *or* 1 package (10 ounces) frozen *asparagus cuts* for the broccoli.

Broccoli-Cheese Chicken

CRISPY CHICKEN WITH ASPARAGUS SAUCE

1 egg *or* 2 egg whites
4 skinless, boneless chicken breast halves *or* 8 skinless, boneless chicken thighs (about 1 pound)
½ cup dry bread crumbs
2 tablespoons vegetable oil
1 can (10¾ ounces) CAMPBELL'S condensed Cream of Asparagus Soup
⅓ cup milk
⅓ cup water
Grated Parmesan cheese
4 cups hot cooked rice
Sweet yellow pepper strips *and* fresh Italian parsley sprig for garnish

■ In shallow dish, beat egg. Dip chicken into egg. On waxed paper, coat chicken with bread crumbs. *(Pictured below.)*

■ In 10-inch skillet over medium-low heat, in hot oil, cook chicken 15 minutes or until browned on both sides and no longer pink. Remove; keep warm. Pour off fat.

■ In same skillet, combine soup, milk and water. Heat through, stirring occasionally. Spoon soup mixture over chicken. Sprinkle with Parmesan cheese. Serve with rice. Garnish with yellow pepper and parsley, if desired.

Makes 4 servings	Prep Time: 10 minutes Cook Time: 20 minutes

Coating chicken

Dip each piece of chicken into egg, allowing excess egg to drip back into dish. Coat both sides of chicken evenly with crumbs, shaking off excess crumbs.

Crispy Chicken with Asparagus Sauce

CHICKEN DIJON

2 tablespoons margarine *or* butter
4 skinless, boneless chicken breast halves (about 1 pound)
1 medium onion, chopped (about ½ cup)
1 can (10¾ ounces) CAMPBELL'S condensed Cream of Mushroom Soup
¼ cup apple juice *or* milk
1 tablespoon chopped fresh parsley *or* 1 teaspoon dried parsley flakes
1 tablespoon Dijon-style mustard
4 cups hot cooked medium egg noodles (about 4 cups dry)
Fresh Italian parsley *and* crab apples for garnish

- In 10-inch skillet over medium-high heat, in *1 tablespoon* hot margarine, cook chicken 10 minutes or until browned on both sides. Remove; set aside.
- Reduce heat to medium. In same skillet, in remaining *1 tablespoon* hot margarine, cook onion until tender, stirring often.
- Stir in soup, apple juice, chopped parsley and mustard. Heat to boiling. Return chicken to skillet. Reduce heat to low. Cover; cook 5 minutes or until chicken is no longer pink, stirring occasionally. Serve with noodles. Garnish with Italian parsley and apples, if desired.

Makes 4 servings	Prep Time: 10 minutes Cook Time: 25 minutes

Before you begin, start heating water to cook the noodles.

Chicken Dijon

CHICKEN–BROCCOLI AU GRATIN

See directions below for making "carrot flowers," as pictured opposite. Or, you may garnish each serving with several carrot curls.

1 can (10¾ ounces) CAMPBELL'S condensed Cream of Chicken & Broccoli Soup
¼ cup milk
4 skinless, boneless chicken breast halves (about 1 pound)
3 tablespoons dry bread crumbs
2 tablespoons grated Parmesan cheese
2 tablespoons margarine *or* butter, melted
Fresh Italian parsley sprigs *and* carrot flowers or carrot curls for garnish

■ In 2-quart oblong baking dish, combine soup and milk. Arrange chicken in soup mixture, turning to coat.

■ In small bowl, combine bread crumbs, Parmesan cheese and margarine. Pat mixture on top of each chicken piece. Bake at 400°F. for 25 minutes or until chicken is no longer pink. Stir sauce; spoon over chicken. Garnish with parsley and carrot flowers, if desired.

Makes 4 servings	Prep Time: 10 minutes Cook Time: 25 minutes

Tip Like radish roses, carrot flowers are easy to make. Select medium carrots for best results. Hold peeled carrot in one hand, with stem end of carrot extending beyond the palm of your hand. Using paring knife, place knife about 3 inches from stem end. To make one "petal," make a diagonal cut toward stem end almost to center of carrot. Working in clockwise direction, make 3 or 4 more diagonal cuts for additional "petals." After cutting, gently twist end of carrot to snap off "carrot flower."

Chicken-Broccoli au Gratin

BAKED CRISPY CHICKEN

Pictured opposite, this herbed chicken entrée is served with steamed, sliced zucchini and sweet yellow pepper strips.

1 can (10¾ ounces) CAMPBELL'S condensed Cream of Chicken Soup
½ cup milk
4 skinless, boneless chicken breast halves (about 1 pound)
2 tablespoons all-purpose flour
1½ cups PEPPERIDGE FARM Herb Seasoned Stuffing, finely crushed
2 tablespoons margarine *or* butter, melted
Fresh rosemary sprigs for garnish

■ In shallow dish, combine ⅓ *cup* soup and ¼ *cup* milk; set aside.

■ On waxed paper, lightly coat chicken with flour; dip into soup mixture. On another piece of waxed paper, coat chicken with stuffing.

■ On baking sheet, arrange chicken. Drizzle with margarine. Bake at 400°F. for 20 minutes or until chicken is no longer pink.

■ Meanwhile, in 1-quart saucepan, combine remaining soup and ¼ *cup* milk. Over medium heat, heat through, stirring occasionally. Serve with chicken. Garnish with rosemary, if desired.

Makes 4 servings	Prep Time: 15 minutes Cook Time: 20 minutes

Tip You may substitute 2 pounds *chicken parts,* skinned, for the boneless chicken. Arrange chicken in 2-quart oblong baking dish. Bake at 375°F. for 1 hour or until chicken is no longer pink and juices run clear.

Baked Crispy Chicken

LEMON ASPARAGUS CHICKEN

1 tablespoon vegetable oil
4 skinless, boneless chicken breast halves (about 1 pound)
1 can (10¾ ounces) CAMPBELL'S condensed Cream of Asparagus Soup
¼ cup milk
1 tablespoon lemon juice
⅛ teaspoon black pepper
4 cups hot cooked linguine (about 8 ounces dry)
Lemon slices *and* cooked fresh asparagus spears for garnish

■ In 10-inch skillet over medium-high heat, in hot oil, cook chicken 10 minutes or until browned on both sides. Remove; set aside. Pour off fat.

■ In same skillet, combine soup, milk, lemon juice and black pepper. Heat to boiling. Return chicken to skillet. Reduce heat to low. Cover; cook 5 minutes or until chicken is no longer pink, stirring occasionally. Serve with linguine. Garnish with lemon slices and asparagus, if desired.

Makes 4 servings	Prep Time: 5 minutes Cook Time: 20 minutes

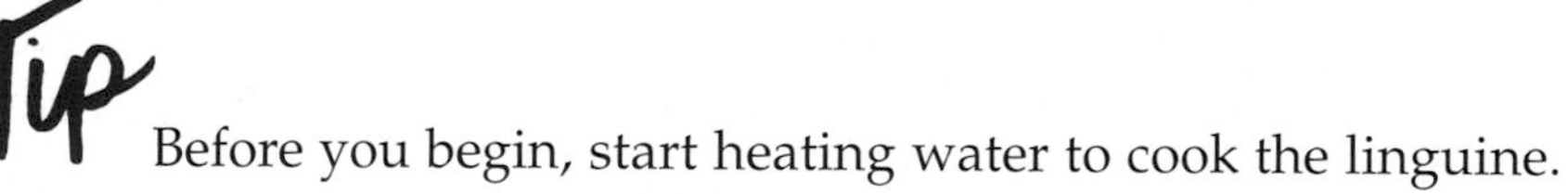

Tip Before you begin, start heating water to cook the linguine.

Lemon Asparagus Chicken

ORIENTAL CHICKEN SKILLET

When fresh beans are in season, you may substitute ½ pound fresh green beans, cut into 2-inch pieces, for the frozen beans.

1 tablespoon vegetable oil
4 skinless, boneless chicken breast halves (about 1 pound)
1 can (10¾ ounces) CAMPBELL'S condensed Cream of Chicken Soup
1 package (9 ounces) frozen cut green beans
2 large green onions, cut into 1-inch pieces (about ½ cup)
⅓ cup water
1 tablespoon soy sauce
¼ teaspoon ground ginger
4 cups hot cooked rice
Fresh plum slices *and* green onion curl for garnish

■ In 10-inch skillet over medium-high heat, in hot oil, cook chicken 10 minutes or until browned on both sides. Remove; set aside. Pour off fat.

■ In same skillet, combine soup, green beans, onion pieces, water, soy sauce and ginger. Heat to boiling. Return chicken to skillet. Reduce heat to low. Cover; cook 5 minutes or until chicken is no longer pink and green beans are tender, stirring occasionally. Serve with rice. Garnish with plum slices and green onion curl, if desired.

Makes 4 servings	Prep Time: 10 minutes Cook Time: 20 minutes

Before you begin, start heating water to cook the rice.

Oriental Chicken Skillet

CRUNCHY CHICKEN BAKE

Pictured opposite, this savory chicken entrée is served with steamed, sliced yellow squash and hot cooked rice. Before you begin, start heating water to cook the rice.

8 skinless, boneless chicken breast halves (about 2 pounds)
4 slices (about 4 ounces) Swiss *or* American cheese, each cut in half
1 can (10¾ ounces) CAMPBELL'S condensed Cream of Broccoli Soup
8 tomato slices
2 tablespoons margarine *or* butter, melted
½ cup PEPPERIDGE FARM Herb Seasoned Stuffing, crushed
8 cups hot cooked rice
Fresh oregano sprigs for garnish

- In 3-quart oblong baking dish, arrange chicken. Top with Swiss cheese.
- In small bowl, stir soup; spread over cheese. (*Pictured below.*) Top with tomatoes. In another small bowl, combine margarine and stuffing; sprinkle over tomatoes.
- Bake at 400°F. for 25 minutes or until chicken is no longer pink. Serve with rice. Garnish with oregano, if desired.

Makes 8 servings	Prep Time: 10 minutes Cook Time: 25 minutes

Assembling casserole

Spoon some of the soup onto one cheese slice. Use rubber spatula to spread soup evenly over cheese and chicken. Repeat with remaining soup.

Crunchy Chicken Bake

ORANGE–GLAZED CHICKEN

For a colorful addition, stir chopped fresh parsley into the hot cooked rice.

1 tablespoon margarine *or* butter
6 skinless, boneless chicken breast halves (about 1½ pounds)
3 tablespoons cornstarch
1 can (14½ ounces) SWANSON Vegetable Broth
½ cup sweet orange marmalade *or* apple jelly
1 teaspoon lemon juice
6 cups hot cooked rice
Fresh thyme sprigs, orange slices *and* chopped, toasted pecans for garnish

■ In 10-inch skillet over medium-high heat, in hot margarine, cook *half* of the chicken 10 minutes or until browned on both sides. Remove; set aside. Repeat with remaining chicken.

■ In small bowl, stir together cornstarch, broth, marmalade and lemon juice until smooth. Add to skillet. Cook until mixture boils and thickens, stirring constantly.

■ Return chicken to skillet. Reduce heat to low. Cook, uncovered, 5 minutes or until chicken is no longer pink, stirring occasionally. Serve with rice. Garnish with thyme, orange slices and pecans, if desired.

Makes 6 servings	Prep Time: 5 minutes Cook Time: 30 minutes

Before you begin, start heating water to cook the rice.

Orange-Glazed Chicken

SHORTCUT BARBECUED CHICKEN

If you like, serve with hot buttered corn on the cob, crusty Italian bread and a garden salad.

1 can (10¾ ounces) CAMPBELL'S condensed Tomato Soup
2 tablespoons honey
1 teaspoon dry mustard
½ teaspoon onion powder
4 chicken breast halves (about 2 pounds), skinned
Fresh Italian parsley sprigs for garnish

■ In medium bowl, combine soup, honey, mustard and onion powder.

■ Arrange chicken, bone side up, on rack in broiler pan. Brush chicken with soup mixture. Broil 6 inches from heat 30 minutes or until no longer pink and juices run clear, turning once and brushing often with soup mixture during cooking. Garnish with parsley, if desired.

Makes 4 servings	Prep Time: 10 minutes Cook Time: 30 minutes

Tip When purchasing chicken, buy about ½ pound bone-in chicken or ¼ pound skinless, boneless chicken for each main-dish serving.

Shortcut Barbecued Chicken

ORIENTAL CHICKEN AND NOODLES

2 tablespoons cornstarch
1 can (14½ ounces) SWANSON Chicken Broth
1 tablespoon soy sauce
2 packages (3 ounces *each*) CAMPBELL'S *or* RAMEN PRIDE Chicken Flavor Ramen Noodle Soup
2 tablespoons vegetable oil
1 pound skinless, boneless chicken breasts, cut into strips
5 cups cut-up fresh vegetables (broccoli, green onions, celery and carrots)
¼ teaspoon ground ginger
⅛ teaspoon garlic powder *or* 1 clove garlic, minced
Fresh enoki mushrooms for garnish

■ In small bowl, stir together cornstarch, broth and soy sauce until smooth; set aside. Cook noodles according to package directions. (Reserve seasoning packets for another use.) Drain off most of liquid; set aside.

■ In 10-inch skillet or wok over medium-high heat, in *1 tablespoon* hot oil, stir-fry *half* of the chicken until browned. Remove; set aside. Repeat with remaining chicken.

■ Reduce heat to medium. In same skillet, in remaining *1 tablespoon* hot oil, stir-fry vegetables, ginger and garlic powder until vegetables are tender-crisp.

■ Add reserved cornstarch mixture. Cook until mixture boils and thickens, stirring constantly. Return chicken to skillet. Heat through, stirring occasionally. Serve over noodles. Pass with additional *soy sauce,* if desired. Garnish with mushrooms, if desired.

Makes 4 servings	**Prep Time: 20 minutes** **Cook Time: 20 minutes**

Oriental Chicken and Noodles

CHICKEN–MUSHROOM RISOTTO

2 tablespoons margarine *or* butter
¾ pound skinless, boneless chicken breasts, cut into cubes
1 cup uncooked regular long-grain rice
1 medium carrot *or* 1 small sweet red pepper, finely chopped (about ⅓ cup)
1 small onion, finely chopped (about ¼ cup)
1 can (14½ ounces) SWANSON Chicken Broth
1 can (10¾ ounces) CAMPBELL'S condensed Cream of Mushroom Soup
⅛ teaspoon black pepper
½ cup frozen peas
Fresh celery leaves *and* carrot curl for garnish

■ In 10-inch skillet or 3-quart saucepan over medium-high heat, in *1 tablespoon* hot margarine, cook chicken until browned, stirring often. Remove; set aside.

■ Reduce heat to medium. In same skillet, in remaining *1 tablespoon* hot margarine, cook rice, chopped carrot and onion until rice is golden brown, stirring constantly. (*Pictured below.*) Stir in broth, soup and black pepper. Heat to boiling. Reduce heat to low. Cover; cook 15 minutes, stirring occasionally.

■ Stir in peas and reserved chicken. Cover; cook 5 minutes more or until rice is tender and liquid is absorbed, stirring occasionally. Garnish with celery leaves and carrot curl, if desired.

Makes about 4½ cups or 4 servings	Prep Time: 10 minutes Cook Time: 35 minutes

Browning rice

In 10-inch skillet, cook rice, carrot and onion until rice is golden brown, stirring constantly.

Chicken-Mushroom Risotto

EASY CHICKEN STROGANOFF

2 tablespoons margarine *or* butter
1 pound skinless, boneless chicken breasts, cut into strips
2 cups sliced fresh mushrooms (about 6 ounces)
1 medium onion, chopped (about ½ cup)
1 can (10¾ ounces) CAMPBELL'S condensed Cream of Chicken Soup
½ cup sour cream *or* plain yogurt
4 cups hot cooked medium egg noodles (about 4 cups dry)
Chopped fresh parsley, paprika, orange peel curls *and* fresh oregano sprigs for garnish

■ In 10-inch skillet over medium-high heat, in *1 tablespoon* hot margarine, cook *half* of the chicken until browned, stirring often. Remove; set aside. Repeat with remaining chicken.

■ Reduce heat to medium. In same skillet, in remaining *1 tablespoon* hot margarine, cook mushrooms and onion until vegetables are tender and liquid is evaporated, stirring often.

■ Stir in soup and sour cream. Heat to boiling. Return chicken to skillet. Heat through, stirring occasionally. Serve over noodles. Sprinkle with parsley and paprika. Garnish with orange peel and oregano, if desired.

Makes 4 servings	**Prep Time: 15 minutes** **Cook Time: 20 minutes**

Easy Turkey Stroganoff: Prepare Easy Chicken Stroganoff as directed above, *except* substitute 1 pound *turkey breast cutlets* or *slices,* cut into thin strips, for the chicken.

Before you begin, start heating water to cook the noodles.

Easy Chicken Stroganoff

BAKED ONION CHICKEN

This three-step recipe bakes in only 20 minutes! Serve with coleslaw, bread sticks and fresh fruit for an extra-easy meal.

1 pouch CAMPBELL'S Dry Onion Soup and Recipe Mix
⅔ cup dry bread crumbs *or* cracker crumbs
⅛ teaspoon black pepper
1 egg *or* 2 egg whites
2 tablespoons water
12 skinless, boneless chicken thighs *or* 6 skinless, boneless chicken breast halves (about 1½ pounds)
2 tablespoons margarine *or* butter, melted (optional)
Orange slices for garnish

■ With rolling pin, crush soup mix in pouch. On waxed paper, combine soup mix, bread crumbs and black pepper.

■ In shallow dish, beat together egg and water. Dip chicken into egg mixture; coat with crumb mixture.

■ On baking sheet, arrange chicken. Drizzle with margarine. Bake at 400°F. for 20 minutes or until chicken is no longer pink. Garnish with orange slices, if desired.

Makes 6 servings	**Prep Time: 10 minutes** **Cook Time: 20 minutes**

For ⅔ cup cracker crumbs, finely crush 16 saltine crackers.

The U.S. Department of Agriculture operates a toll-free Meat and Poultry Hotline to answer your food safety questions about meat and poultry. From 10 a.m. to 4 p.m. Eastern Standard Time, Monday through Friday, home economists will answer your meat and poultry questions—just dial 1-800-535-4555. If you are in the Washington, DC metropolitan area, dial (202) 720-3333.*

*Source: U.S. Department of Agriculture–Food Safety and Inspection Service.

Baked Onion Chicken

SKILLET BROCCOLI CHICKEN

Ready in less than 30 minutes, this quick-to-fix recipe features Cream of Chicken & Broccoli Soup.

1 tablespoon vegetable oil
4 skinless, boneless chicken breast halves (about 1 pound)
1 can (10¾ ounces) CAMPBELL'S condensed Cream of Chicken & Broccoli Soup
½ cup milk
⅛ teaspoon black pepper
4 cups hot cooked rice
Chopped fresh parsley, carrot curls *and* apple wedges for garnish

■ In 10-inch skillet over medium-high heat, in hot oil, cook chicken 10 minutes or until browned on both sides. Remove; set aside. Pour off fat.

■ In same skillet, combine soup, milk and black pepper. Heat to boiling. Return chicken to skillet. Reduce heat to low. Cover; cook 5 minutes or until chicken is no longer pink, stirring occasionally. Serve with rice. Sprinkle with parsley; garnish with carrot curls and apple wedges, if desired.

Makes 4 servings	Prep Time: 5 minutes Cook Time: 20 minutes

Before you begin, start heating water to cook the rice.

Skillet Broccoli Chicken

CHICKEN QUESADILLAS

- **1 can (10¾ ounces) CAMPBELL'S condensed Cream of Chicken Soup**
- **1½ cups chopped cooked chicken**
- **1 cup shredded Cheddar cheese (4 ounces)**
- **1 fresh *or* canned jalapeño pepper, seeded and finely chopped (about 1 tablespoon), optional**
- **8 flour tortillas (8 inches *each*)**
- **PACE Thick & Chunky Salsa**
- **Sour cream**
- **Fresh plum tomato slices, jalapeño pepper slices *and* fresh cilantro sprigs for garnish**

■ In small bowl, combine soup, chicken, ½ *cup* Cheddar cheese and chopped jalapeño pepper.

■ Top *half* of each tortilla with ¼ *cup* soup mixture, spreading evenly to within ½ inch of edge. Moisten edges of tortillas with water; fold over, pressing edges to seal. (*Pictured below.*) On 2 large baking sheets, arrange filled tortillas.

■ Bake at 400°F. for 8 minutes or until hot. Sprinkle with remaining ½ *cup* Cheddar cheese. Serve with salsa and sour cream. Garnish with tomato, jalapeño pepper slices and cilantro, if desired.

Makes 8 quesadillas or 4 servings	**Prep Time: 15 minutes Cook Time: 8 minutes**

Assembling quesadillas

Lightly moisten edges of tortillas. Fold tortillas to enclose filling. Press moistened edges to seal.

Chicken Quesadillas

SAVORY CHICKEN AND MUSHROOMS

2 tablespoons margarine *or* butter
4 skinless, boneless chicken breast halves (about 1 pound)
1½ cups fresh broccoli flowerets
1½ cups sliced fresh mushrooms (about 4 ounces)
1 can (10¾ ounces) CAMPBELL'S condensed Cream of Chicken & Broccoli Soup
¼ cup milk
2 tablespoons Dijon-style mustard
4 cups hot cooked medium egg noodles (about 4 cups dry)
Red grapes *and* fresh sage leaves for garnish

■ In 10-inch skillet over medium-high heat, in *1 tablespoon* hot margarine, cook chicken 10 minutes or until browned on both sides. Remove; set aside.

■ Reduce heat to medium. In same skillet, in remaining *1 tablespoon* hot margarine, cook broccoli and mushrooms until vegetables are tender and liquid is evaporated, stirring often.

■ Stir in soup, milk and mustard. Heat to boiling. Return chicken to skillet. Reduce heat to low. Cover; cook 5 minutes or until chicken is no longer pink, stirring occasionally. Serve with noodles. Garnish with grapes and sage, if desired.

Makes 4 servings	Prep Time: 10 minutes Cook Time: 25 minutes

Before you begin, start heating water to cook the noodles.

Savory Chicken and Mushrooms

TURKEY–BROCCOLI DIVAN

Made with either turkey or chicken, this shortcut divan is one of Campbell's most requested recipes. If you like, the recipe may be doubled and baked in a 3-quart oblong baking dish.

1 pound fresh broccoli, cut into spears *or* 1 package (10 ounces) frozen broccoli spears, cooked and drained
1½ cups cubed cooked turkey *or* chicken
1 can (10¾ ounces) CAMPBELL'S condensed Cream of Broccoli Soup
⅓ cup milk
½ cup shredded Cheddar cheese (2 ounces)
2 tablespoons dry bread crumbs
1 tablespoon margarine *or* butter, melted
Green grapes, fresh parsley sprigs *and* thin Cheddar cheese bread sticks for garnish

■ In 9-inch pie plate or 2-quart oblong baking dish, arrange broccoli and turkey. In small bowl, combine soup and milk; pour over broccoli and turkey.

■ Sprinkle Cheddar cheese over soup mixture. In cup, combine bread crumbs and margarine; sprinkle over cheese.

■ Bake at 450°F. for 20 minutes or until hot and bubbling. Garnish with grapes, parsley and bread sticks, if desired.

Makes 4 servings	Prep Time: 15 minutes Cook Time: 20 minutes

Tip You may substitute 2 cans (5 ounces *each*) SWANSON *Premium Chunk White Turkey, Chunk White Chicken* or *Chunk Chicken* for the cubed cooked turkey.

Turkey-Broccoli Divan

TURKEY–NOODLE PARMESAN

All you need is a colorful garden salad and crusty garlic bread to round out this creamy one-dish entrée.

3 cups dry medium egg noodles
1 can (10¾ ounces) CAMPBELL'S condensed Cream of Chicken Soup
½ cup milk
⅓ cup grated Parmesan cheese
⅛ teaspoon black pepper
2 cups cubed cooked turkey *or* chicken
Chopped fresh parsley *and* red onion strips for garnish

■ In 3-quart saucepan, prepare noodles according to package directions. Drain in colander.

■ In same saucepan, combine soup, milk, Parmesan cheese and black pepper; add noodles and turkey. Over low heat, heat through, stirring occasionally. Sprinkle with parsley and additional Parmesan cheese; garnish with onion strips, if desired.

Makes about 4½ cups or 4 servings	Prep Time: 20 minutes Cook Time: 10 minutes

Tip You may substitute 2 cans (5 ounces *each*) SWANSON *Premium Chunk White Turkey, Chunk White Chicken* or *Chunk Chicken* for the cubed cooked turkey.

Turkey-Noodle Parmesan

TURKEY–VEGETABLE STIR–FRY

To save time, slice the carrots while heating water to cook the rice.

2 tablespoons vegetable oil
1 pound turkey breast cutlets *or* slices, cut into strips
4 medium carrots, thinly sliced (about 1⅓ cups)
¼ teaspoon ground ginger (optional)
1 can (10¾ ounces) CAMPBELL'S condensed Cream of Celery Soup
2 medium green onions, sliced (about ¼ cup)
3 tablespoons water
1 tablespoon soy sauce
4 cups hot cooked rice
Green onion top *and* carrot curl for garnish

■ In 10-inch skillet or wok over medium-high heat, in *1 tablespoon* hot oil, stir-fry *half* of the turkey until browned. Remove; set aside. Repeat with remaining turkey.

■ Reduce heat to medium. In same skillet, in remaining *1 tablespoon* hot oil, stir-fry sliced carrots and ginger until carrots are tender-crisp.

■ Stir in soup, sliced onions, water and soy sauce. Heat to boiling. Return turkey to skillet. Heat through, stirring occasionally. Serve over rice. Garnish with green onion top and carrot curl, if desired.

Makes 4 servings	**Prep Time: 15 minutes** **Cook Time: 20 minutes**

Chicken-Vegetable Stir-Fry: Prepare Turkey-Vegetable Stir-Fry as directed above, *except* substitute 1 pound *skinless, boneless chicken breasts,* cut into thin strips, for the turkey.

Slicing turkey for stir-frying

Turkey cutlets are cut from the turkey breast. Shown here, the cutlets are sliced, across the grain, into thin strips.

Turkey-Vegetable Stir-Fry

SKILLET TURKEY AND ASPARAGUS

1 tablespoon vegetable oil
1 pound turkey breast cutlets *or* slices
1 can (10¾ ounces) CAMPBELL'S condensed Cream of Asparagus Soup
¾ pound fresh asparagus spears (12 to 15), trimmed and cut into 2-inch pieces (about 1½ cups) *or* 1 package (10 ounces) frozen asparagus cuts
⅓ cup milk
⅛ teaspoon black pepper
4 cups hot cooked rice
Green onion curls *and* orange slices for garnish

■ In 10-inch skillet over medium-high heat, in hot oil, cook *half* of the turkey 3 minutes or until browned on both sides. Remove; set aside. Repeat with remaining turkey. Pour off fat.

■ In same skillet, combine soup, asparagus, milk and black pepper. Heat to boiling. Return turkey to skillet. Reduce heat to low. Cover; cook 5 minutes or until turkey is no longer pink and asparagus is tender, stirring occasionally. Serve with rice. Garnish with onion curls and orange slices, if desired.

Makes 4 servings	Prep Time: 10 minutes Cook Time: 16 minutes

Skillet Chicken and Asparagus: Prepare Skillet Turkey and Asparagus as directed above, *except* substitute 4 *skinless, boneless chicken breast halves* (about 1 pound) for the turkey. Cook chicken breasts 10 minutes or until browned on both sides. After returning chicken to skillet, increase cooking time to 10 minutes.

Tip Before you begin, start heating water to cook the rice.

Skillet Turkey and Asparagus

Blue-Ribbon Beef & Pork

BEEF AND MOZZARELLA BAKE

Pictured opposite, this Italian-style casserole is served with a sliced tomato salad and crusty garlic bread.

1 pound ground beef
1 can (11⅛ ounces) CAMPBELL'S condensed Italian Tomato Soup
1 can (10¾ ounces) CAMPBELL'S condensed Cream of Mushroom Soup
1¼ cups water
1 teaspoon dried basil leaves, crushed
¼ teaspoon black pepper
⅛ teaspoon garlic powder *or* 1 clove garlic, minced
1½ cups shredded mozzarella cheese (6 ounces)
4 cups cooked medium shell macaroni (about 3 cups dry)

■ In 10-inch skillet over medium-high heat, cook beef until browned, stirring to separate meat. Spoon off fat.

■ Stir in soups, water, basil, black pepper, garlic powder and *1 cup* mozzarella cheese; add macaroni. In 2-quart oblong baking dish, spoon mixture. Bake at 400°F. for 25 minutes or until hot and bubbling. Stir. Sprinkle with remaining *½ cup* mozzarella cheese. Bake 5 minutes or until cheese is melted.

Makes about 8 cups or 6 servings	**Prep Time: 15 minutes Cook Time: 30 minutes**

Tip Before you begin, start heating water to cook the macaroni. And, you may substitute 4 cups cooked *elbow macaroni* (about 2 cups dry) for the shell macaroni.

Beef and Mozzarella Bake

GINGER–BEEF STIR–FRY

To save time, cut up the vegetables while cooking the rice.

1 pound boneless beef sirloin *or* top round steak, ¾ inch thick
2 tablespoons cornstarch
1 can (14½ ounces) SWANSON Beef Broth
2 tablespoons soy sauce
2 tablespoons vegetable oil
5 cups cut-up fresh vegetables (green pepper, carrot, mushrooms, celery and onion)
1 teaspoon ground ginger
¼ teaspoon garlic powder *or* 2 cloves garlic, minced
4 cups hot cooked rice
Fresh sage leaves *and* kumquat or orange slices for garnish

- Slice beef, across the grain, into thin strips; set aside. *(Pictured below.)* In small bowl, stir together cornstarch, broth and soy sauce until smooth; set aside.
- In 10-inch skillet or wok over medium-high heat, in *1 tablespoon* hot oil, stir-fry *half* of the beef until browned. Remove; set aside. Repeat with remaining beef.
- Reduce heat to medium. In same skillet, in remaining *1 tablespoon* hot oil, stir-fry vegetables, ginger and garlic powder until vegetables are tender-crisp.
- Stir in reserved cornstarch mixture. Cook until mixture boils and thickens, stirring constantly. Return beef to skillet. Heat through, stirring occasionally. Serve over rice. Garnish with sage and kumquat, if desired.

Makes about 6 cups or 4 servings	Prep Time: 20 minutes Cook Time: 20 minutes

Slicing beef for stir-frying

To make slicing easier, freeze beef for 1 hour. Slice beef, across the grain, into thin strips.

Ginger-Beef Stir-Fry

SKILLET MAC 'N' BEEF

Quick and easy—just add a zesty garden salad and garlic bread and supper is ready in 25 minutes!

1 pound ground beef
1 medium onion, chopped (about ½ cup)
1 can (10¾ ounces) CAMPBELL'S condensed Cream of Celery Soup
¼ cup ketchup
1 tablespoon Worcestershire sauce
2 cups cooked corkscrew macaroni (about 1½ cups dry)
Fresh basil leaves *and* cherry tomato halves for garnish

■ In 10-inch skillet over medium-high heat, cook beef and onion until beef is browned and onion is tender, stirring to separate meat. Spoon off fat.

■ Stir in soup, ketchup and Worcestershire sauce; add macaroni. Reduce heat to low. Heat through, stirring occasionally. Garnish with basil and cherry tomato halves, if desired.

Makes about 4½ cups or 4 servings	Prep Time: 10 minutes Cook Time: 15 minutes

Tip Before you begin, start heating water to cook the macaroni. And, you may substitute 2 cups cooked *elbow macaroni* (about 1 cup dry) for the corkscrew macaroni.

Skillet Mac 'n' Beef

CHILI CON CARNE

This spicy chili also makes a great-tasting potato topper.
See directions below for micro-cooked potatoes.

1 pound ground beef
1 medium green pepper, chopped (about ¾ cup)
1 can (about 15 ounces) kidney beans, rinsed and drained
1 can (11⅛ ounces) CAMPBELL'S condensed Italian Tomato Soup
¾ cup water
2 tablespoons chili powder
1 tablespoon vinegar
Tortilla chips, sour cream *and* fresh cilantro sprigs for garnish

■ In 10-inch skillet over medium-high heat, cook beef and green pepper until beef is browned and pepper is tender, stirring to separate meat. Spoon off fat.

■ Stir in beans, soup, water, chili powder and vinegar. Heat to boiling. Reduce heat to low. Cook, uncovered, 15 minutes, stirring occasionally. Garnish with tortilla chips, sour cream and cilantro, if desired. Sprinkle with additional chili powder, if desired.

Makes about 4 cups or 4 servings	Prep Time: 10 minutes Cook Time: 25 minutes

Chili con Carne and Potatoes: Prepare Chili con Carne as directed above, *except* spoon mixture over 8 split, hot *baked potatoes.* Makes 8 side-dish servings.

Tip Scrub 8 potatoes (8 ounces *each*); pierce each potato with fork several times. Arrange *4 potatoes* in circle on microwave-safe plate. Microwave, uncovered, on HIGH for 10½ to 12½ minutes, rearranging potatoes once during cooking. Let stand a few minutes before serving. Repeat with remaining potatoes. (For oven-baked potatoes, see directions on page 90.)

Chili con Carne

SOUPERBURGER SANDWICHES

This 20-minute skillet supper is guaranteed to get you out of the kitchen fast!

1 pound ground beef
1 medium onion, chopped (about ½ cup)
1 can (10¾ ounces) CAMPBELL'S condensed Cheddar Cheese Soup
2 tablespoons ketchup
⅛ teaspoon black pepper
6 hamburger buns, split and toasted

■ In 10-inch skillet over medium-high heat, cook beef and onion until beef is browned and onion is tender, stirring to separate meat. Spoon off fat.

■ Stir in soup, ketchup and black pepper. Reduce heat to low. Heat through, stirring occasionally. Serve on buns.

Makes about 3 cups or 6 servings	Prep Time: 5 minutes Cook Time: 15 minutes

Tip Next time, substitute 1 can (10¾ ounces) CAMPBELL'S condensed *Cream of Celery Soup* for the Cheddar Cheese Soup and 1 tablespoon *prepared mustard* for the ketchup.

Souperburger Sandwiches

BROCCOLI–BEEF STIR–FRY

To save time, prepare quick-cooking white or brown rice while stir-frying the beef.

1 pound boneless beef sirloin *or* top round steak, ¾ inch thick
2 tablespoons vegetable oil
2 cups fresh broccoli flowerets
½ teaspoon ground ginger
¼ teaspoon garlic powder *or* 2 cloves garlic, minced
1 can (10¾ ounces) CAMPBELL'S condensed Tomato Soup
2 tablespoons soy sauce
1 tablespoon vinegar
4 cups hot cooked rice
Fresh herb sprigs *and* sweet yellow pepper strips for garnish

- Slice beef, across the grain, into thin strips *(see photo, page 52)*.
- In 10-inch skillet or wok over medium-high heat, in *1 tablespoon* hot oil, stir-fry *half* of the beef until browned. Remove; set aside. Repeat with remaining beef.
- Reduce heat to medium. In same skillet, in remaining *1 tablespoon* hot oil, stir-fry broccoli, ginger and garlic powder until broccoli is tender-crisp.
- Stir in soup, soy sauce and vinegar. Heat to boiling. Return beef to skillet. Heat through, stirring occasionally. Serve over rice. Garnish with herb sprigs and yellow pepper, if desired.

Makes about 3 cups or 4 servings	Prep Time: 10 minutes Cook Time: 20 minutes

Cutting broccoli into flowerets

Remove outer leaves. Trim tough parts of broccoli stalks. Cut into bite-size pieces called flowerets.

Broccoli-Beef Stir-Fry

SAVORY PORK AND VEGETABLES

This entrée is ideal to serve family and friends alike. Pictured opposite, the tender chops are served with buttered carrots and petite croissants. Bon appétit!

2 tablespoons margarine *or* butter
4 boneless pork chops, each ¾ inch thick (about 1 pound)
1½ cups sliced fresh mushrooms (about 4 ounces)
½ teaspoon dried rosemary leaves, crushed
1 can (10¾ ounces) CAMPBELL'S condensed Cream of Mushroom Soup
½ pound fresh sugar snap peas (about 1½ cups) *or* 1 package (10 ounces) frozen sugar snap peas
2 tablespoons water
4 cups hot cooked medium egg noodles (about 4 cups dry)
Snipped fresh rosemary for garnish

■ In 10-inch skillet over medium-high heat, in *1 tablespoon* hot margarine, cook chops 10 minutes or until browned on both sides. Remove; set aside.

■ Reduce heat to medium. In same skillet, in remaining *1 tablespoon* hot margarine, cook mushrooms and dried rosemary until mushrooms are tender and liquid is evaporated, stirring often.

■ Stir in soup, peas and water. Heat to boiling. Return chops to skillet. Reduce heat to low. Cover; cook 10 minutes or until chops are no longer pink and peas are tender, stirring occasionally. Serve with noodles. Sprinkle with fresh rosemary, if desired.

Makes 4 servings	Prep Time: 10 minutes Cook Time: 30 minutes

Tip You may substitute ½ pound fresh *green beans,* cut into 2-inch pieces (about 1½ cups), *or* 1 package (9 ounces) frozen *cut green beans* for the sugar snap peas.

Savory Pork and Vegetables

TOMATO–HERBED PORK CHOPS

Either rib or loin pork chops may be used to make this saucy skillet entrée.

3 recipes Vegetable-Seasoned Rice (see recipe, page 84) ***or*** **6 cups hot cooked rice**
2 tablespoons all-purpose flour
¼ teaspoon dried thyme leaves, crushed
6 pork chops, each ¾ inch thick (about 2 pounds)
1 tablespoon vegetable oil
1 can (10¾ ounces) CAMPBELL'S condensed Tomato Soup
1 medium onion, sliced and separated into rings (about ½ cup)
¼ cup water
Small kale leaves for garnish

■ Prepare Vegetable-Seasoned Rice as directed. Meanwhile, on waxed paper, combine flour and thyme. Lightly coat chops with flour mixture.

■ In 10-inch skillet over medium-high heat, in hot oil, cook *half* of the chops 10 minutes or until browned on both sides. Remove; set aside. Repeat with remaining chops. Pour off fat.

■ In same skillet, combine soup, onion and water. Heat to boiling. Return chops to skillet. Reduce heat to low. Cover; cook 10 minutes or until chops are no longer pink, stirring occasionally. Serve with Vegetable-Seasoned Rice. Garnish with kale, if desired.

Makes 6 servings	Prep Time: 5 minutes Cook Time: 35 minutes

Tip Kale has frilly, dark green leaves and is available year-round. Eaten raw or cooked, it has a mild, cabbagelike flavor. Use kale leaves as you would fresh spinach. But before using, remove the tough center stalks from the leaves. Ornamental kale, as shown in the photo opposite, has smaller leaves and comes in colors ranging from lavender to dark purple and light green to dark green.

Tomato-Herbed Pork Chops ***and*** **Vegetable-Seasoned Rice**

PORK AND CORN STUFFING BAKE

1 can (10¾ ounces) CAMPBELL'S condensed Cream of Celery Soup
1½ cups PEPPERIDGE FARM Corn Bread Stuffing
½ cup cooked whole kernel corn
1 small onion, finely chopped (about ¼ cup)
¼ cup finely chopped celery
½ teaspoon paprika
4 boneless pork chops, each ¾ inch thick (about 1 pound)
1 tablespoon packed brown sugar
1 teaspoon spicy brown mustard

■ In medium bowl, combine soup, stuffing, corn, onion, celery and paprika. In 9-inch greased pie plate, spoon stuffing mixture. Arrange chops on stuffing mixture, pressing lightly into stuffing.

■ In cup, combine sugar and mustard. Spread mixture over chops.

■ Bake at 400°F. for 30 minutes or until chops are no longer pink. Transfer chops to serving platter. Stir stuffing; serve with chops. Sprinkle with additional paprika, if desired.

Makes 4 servings	**Prep Time: 15 minutes** **Cook Time: 30 minutes**

Pork and Fruited Stuffing Bake: Prepare Pork and Corn Stuffing Bake as directed above, *except* add ⅓ cup *raisins* or *chopped mixed dried fruit* with the stuffing.

Chopping onions

What's the difference? *Cubing* means to cut a food into uniform pieces, usually about ½ inch on all sides. *Chopping* refers to cutting a food into irregular pieces about the size of peas. *Finely chopping* refers to chopping a food into tiny irregular pieces.

Pork and Corn Stuffing Bake

PORK MOZZARELLA

Pictured opposite, these savory chops are served with steamed baby sunburst squash, baby zucchini and hot parslied linguine.

1 pouch CAMPBELL'S Dry Onion Soup and Recipe Mix
⅓ cup dry bread crumbs *or* cracker crumbs
⅛ teaspoon black pepper
1 egg *or* 2 egg whites
2 tablespoons water
6 boneless pork chops, each ¾ inch thick (about 1½ pounds)
1½ cups PREGO Traditional Spaghetti Sauce
1 cup shredded mozzarella cheese (4 ounces)

■ With rolling pin, crush soup mix in pouch. On waxed paper, combine soup mix, bread crumbs and black pepper.

■ In shallow dish, beat together egg and water. Dip chops into egg mixture; coat with soup mixture.

■ In 2-quart oblong baking dish, arrange chops. Bake at 400°F. for 20 minutes.

■ Pour spaghetti sauce over chops. Sprinkle with mozzarella cheese. Bake 5 minutes more or until chops are no longer pink and sauce is hot and bubbling.

Makes 6 servings	Prep Time: 10 minutes Cook Time: 25 minutes

Tip You may substitute 6 *pork chops,* bone in and each ¾ inch thick (about 2 pounds), for the boneless chops. Use 3-quart oblong baking dish. Increase cooking time to 30 minutes.

Pork Mozzarella

Sensational Pasta, Vegetables & More

CHEDDARY PASTA AND VEGETABLES

1½ cups dry corkscrew macaroni
1 cup fresh broccoli flowerets
2 medium carrots, sliced (about 1 cup)
1 large sweet red *or* green pepper, coarsely chopped (about 1 cup), optional
1 can (10¾ ounces) CAMPBELL'S condensed Cream of Celery Soup
½ cup shredded Cheddar cheese (2 ounces)
½ cup milk
1 tablespoon prepared mustard

■ In 4-quart saucepan, prepare macaroni according to package directions. Add broccoli, carrots and red pepper for last 5 minutes of cooking time. Drain in colander.

■ In same saucepan, combine soup, Cheddar cheese, milk and mustard. Over low heat, heat until cheese is melted, stirring often. Add macaroni and vegetables. Heat through, stirring occasionally.

Makes about 4½ cups or 5 servings	Prep Time: 10 minutes Cook Time: 20 minutes

Before you begin, start heating water to cook the macaroni.

Cheddary Pasta and Vegetables

GLAZED VEGETABLES

Celery grows in bunches called stalks. Each stalk consists of many "ribs" with leafy green tops. The tender center is commonly referred to as the "heart."

2 tablespoons cornstarch
1 can (14½ ounces) SWANSON Vegetable Broth
2 medium carrots, sliced (about 1 cup)
2 ribs celery, sliced (about 1 cup)
1 medium sweet red pepper, cut into strips (about 1 cup)
1 large onion, cut into wedges (about 1 cup)
1 cup fresh broccoli flowerets
1 cup fresh snow peas (about 4 ounces), trimmed
½ teaspoon ground ginger
¼ teaspoon garlic powder *or* 2 cloves garlic, minced

■ In cup, stir together cornstarch and *¼ cup* broth until smooth; set aside.

■ In 10-inch skillet or wok over medium-high heat, heat remaining broth, carrots, celery, red pepper, onion, broccoli, snow peas, ginger and garlic powder to boiling.

■ Add reserved cornstarch mixture. Cook until mixture boils and thickens, stirring constantly.

■ Reduce heat to medium. Cover; cook 5 minutes or until vegetables are tender, stirring occasionally.

Makes about 4 cups or 4 servings	Prep Time: 15 minutes Cook Time: 15 minutes

Cutting onions into wedges

Cut peeled onion in half, from stem to root end. Place cut sides up on cutting board. Cut in half again to make large wedges. Continue cutting to yield 4 to 6 wedges from each onion half.

Glazed Vegetables

VEGETABLE–RICE PILAF

- 1 tablespoon margarine *or* butter
- ¾ cup uncooked regular long-grain rice
- ¼ teaspoon dried basil leaves, crushed
- 1 can (14½ ounces) SWANSON Vegetable Broth
- ¾ cup frozen peas and carrots
- ¼ cup chopped sweet red pepper
- Fresh basil leaves for garnish

■ In 2-quart saucepan over medium-high heat, in hot margarine, cook rice and dried basil until rice is browned, stirring constantly.

■ Stir in broth. Heat to boiling. Reduce heat to low. Cover; cook 10 minutes. Add peas and carrots and red pepper. Cover; cook 10 minutes or until rice is tender and liquid is absorbed. Garnish with fresh basil, if desired.

Makes about 3½ cups or 4 servings	Prep Time: 5 minutes Cook Time: 25 minutes

BROCCOLI AND NOODLES SUPREME

- 3 cups dry medium egg noodles
- 2 cups fresh broccoli flowerets
- 1 can (10¾ ounces) CAMPBELL'S condensed Cream of Chicken & Broccoli Soup
- ½ cup sour cream
- ⅓ cup grated Parmesan cheese
- ⅛ teaspoon black pepper
- Diced carrot *and* sweet red pepper strips for garnish

■ In 4-quart saucepan, prepare noodles according to package directions. Add broccoli for last 5 minutes of cooking time. Drain in colander.

■ In same saucepan, combine soup, sour cream, Parmesan cheese and black pepper; add noodles and broccoli. Over low heat, heat through, stirring occasionally. Garnish with diced carrot and red pepper, if desired.

Makes about 4 cups or 5 servings	Prep Time: 5 minutes Cook Time: 20 minutes

Vegetable-Rice Pilaf (top) *and*
Broccoli and Noodles Supreme (bottom)

NEW POTATOES AND PEAS

New potatoes are simply young potatoes of any variety. They are usually small in size and have not been stored for a long period of time. In this recipe, use small round white or round red thin-skinned potatoes.

9 small new potatoes (about 1½ pounds), quartered (about 4 cups)
1 can (10¾ ounces) CAMPBELL'S condensed Cream of Mushroom Soup
⅓ cup milk
½ teaspoon dried dill weed *or* thyme leaves, crushed
⅛ teaspoon black pepper
1 package (10 ounces) frozen peas with pearl onions *or* peas, thawed and drained
Fresh dill sprig *and* lemon wedge for garnish

■ In 4-quart saucepan, place potatoes. Add water to cover potatoes. Over high heat, heat to boiling. Reduce heat to medium. Cook 8 minutes or until potatoes are fork-tender. Drain in colander.

■ In same saucepan, combine soup, milk, dill weed and black pepper. Add potatoes and peas with pearl onions. Over low heat, heat through, stirring occasionally. Garnish with fresh dill and lemon wedge, if desired.

Makes about 5½ cups or 7 servings	Prep Time: 10 minutes Cook Time: 20 minutes

New Potatoes and Peas

VEGETABLE ROTINI

When time is short, substitute 1 bag (16 ounces) frozen vegetable combination for the fresh broccoli, cauliflower and carrots.

2½ cups dry rotini *or* corkscrew macaroni
1½ cups fresh broccoli flowerets
1½ cups fresh cauliflowerets
2 medium carrots, cut into strips (about 1 cup)
1 can (10¾ ounces) CAMPBELL'S condensed Broccoli Cheese Soup
1 package (3 ounces) cream cheese *or* cream cheese with chives, softened
¾ cup milk
½ cup grated Parmesan cheese
2 tablespoons Dijon-style mustard (optional)
⅛ teaspoon black pepper

■ In 4-quart saucepan, prepare rotini according to package directions. Add broccoli, cauliflower and carrots for last 5 minutes of cooking time. Drain in colander.

■ In same saucepan, gradually stir soup into cream cheese; add milk, Parmesan cheese, mustard and black pepper. Over low heat, heat until cream cheese is melted, stirring often. Add macaroni and vegetables. Heat through, stirring occasionally.

Makes about 6 cups or 6 servings	Prep Time: 15 minutes Cook Time: 20 minutes

Cutting carrots into strips

Cut carrot crosswise into thirds. Cut each third in half lengthwise. With cut side down, cut lengthwise into ¼-inch slices. Stack slices and cut again, lengthwise, into thin strips.

Vegetable Rotini

MUSHROOM–BROCCOLI ALFREDO

If you like, accompany this vegetable and pasta combination with grilled chicken brushed with melted margarine and sprinkled with snipped fresh rosemary and cracked black pepper. (Pictured opposite.)

2 tablespoons margarine *or* butter
3 cups fresh broccoli flowerets
3 cups fresh sliced mushrooms (about 8 ounces)
1 medium onion, coarsely chopped (about ½ cup)
¼ teaspoon garlic powder *or* 2 cloves garlic, minced
1 can (10¾ ounces) CAMPBELL'S condensed Cream of Mushroom Soup
⅓ cup milk *or* Chablis *or* other dry white wine
2 tablespoons grated Parmesan cheese
⅛ teaspoon black pepper
4 cups hot cooked fettuccine *or* spaghetti (about 8 ounces dry)
Celery leaves, lemon slices *and* tomato rose for garnish

■ In 10-inch skillet over medium heat, in hot margarine, cook broccoli, mushrooms, onion and garlic powder until vegetables are tender-crisp and liquid is evaporated, stirring often.

■ Stir in soup, milk, Parmesan cheese and black pepper. Heat through, stirring occasionally. Serve over fettuccine. Garnish with celery leaves, lemon slices and tomato rose, if desired.

Makes about 3 cups sauce or 4 servings	Prep Time: 15 minutes Cook Time: 15 minutes

Tip For cutting broccoli into flowerets, see photo and directions on page 60.

Mushroom-Broccoli Alfredo

SKILLET BASIL POTATOES

If fresh basil is available, finely snip enough leaves to make 1½ teaspoons. Omit dried basil. Stir in fresh basil with the soup, cheese and water.

1 tablespoon margarine *or* butter
1 small onion, chopped (about ¼ cup)
½ teaspoon dried basil leaves, crushed
1 can (10¾ ounces) CAMPBELL'S condensed Cream of Celery Soup
½ cup shredded Cheddar cheese (2 ounces)
¼ cup water
4 medium potatoes (about 1¼ pounds), cooked and sliced (about 4 cups)
Fresh basil leaves *and* cherry tomato wedges for garnish

■ In 10-inch skillet over medium heat, in hot margarine, cook onion and dried basil until onion is tender, stirring occasionally.

■ Stir in soup, Cheddar cheese and water. Reduce heat to low. Heat until cheese is melted, stirring often. Add potatoes. Heat through, stirring occasionally. *(Pictured below.)* Garnish with fresh basil and tomato, if desired.

Makes about 4 cups or 4 servings	Prep Time: 20 minutes Cook Time: 15 minutes

Heating potatoes

Add cooked potatoes to soup mixture. Heat through, gently stirring with wooden spoon, being careful not to break up potatoes.

Skillet Basil Potatoes

VEGETABLE–SEASONED RICE

A tasty accompaniment to pork or poultry. (Pictured on page 65.)

1 can (14½ ounces) SWANSON Vegetable Broth
¾ cup uncooked regular long-grain rice
Fresh herb sprigs for garnish

■ In 2-quart saucepan over medium-high heat, heat broth to boiling. Stir in rice.

■ Reduce heat to low. Cover; cook 20 minutes or until rice is tender and liquid is absorbed. Garnish with herb sprigs, if desired.

Makes about 2 cups or 4 servings	Prep Time: 5 minutes Cook Time: 25 minutes

SAUCY ASPARAGUS

1 can (10¾ ounces) CAMPBELL'S condensed Cream of Asparagus Soup
2 tablespoons milk
1½ pounds fresh asparagus spears (24 to 30), trimmed and cut into 1-inch pieces (about 3 cups) *or* 2 packages (10 ounces *each*) frozen asparagus cuts
Fresh herb sprig *and* lemon slice for garnish

■ In 2-quart saucepan, combine soup and milk. Over medium heat, heat to boiling, stirring occasionally.

■ Add asparagus. Reduce heat to low. Cover; cook 10 minutes or until asparagus is tender, stirring occasionally. Garnish with herb sprig and lemon slice, if desired.

Makes about 3 cups or 6 servings	Prep Time: 10 minutes Cook Time: 15 minutes

Vegetable-Seasoned Rice (top) *and* Saucy Asparagus (bottom)

CREAMY CHICKEN–BROCCOLI RICE

1 can (10¾ ounces) CAMPBELL'S condensed Cream of Chicken & Broccoli Soup
1½ cups water
⅛ teaspoon black pepper
¾ cup uncooked regular long-grain rice
Sweet orange pepper strips, radish wedges *and* fresh parsley sprigs for garnish

- In 2-quart saucepan, combine soup, water and black pepper. Over medium-high heat, heat to boiling.
- Stir in rice. Reduce heat to low. Cover; cook 25 minutes or until rice is tender and mixture is creamy, stirring often. Garnish with orange pepper strips, radish and parsley, if desired.

Makes about 3 cups or 6 servings	Prep Time: 5 minutes Cook Time: 30 minutes

STEAMED VEGETABLES

1 can (14½ ounces) SWANSON Vegetable Broth
3 cups cut-up fresh vegetables (broccoli, carrots, cauliflower and celery) *or* 1 bag (16 ounces) frozen vegetable combination

- In 2-quart saucepan over medium-high heat, heat broth and vegetables to boiling. Reduce heat to low. Cover; cook 5 minutes or until vegetables are tender. Drain.

Makes about 2½ cups or 4 servings	Prep Time: 10 minutes Cook Time: 10 minutes

Tip Reserve broth after vegetables are cooked (about 1½ cups) and use in place of water to prepare rice. In 1-quart saucepan over medium-high heat, heat broth to boiling. Add ½ cup uncooked regular long-grain rice. Cover; cook according to package directions. Makes about 1½ cups or 3 servings.

Creamy Chicken-Broccoli Rice (top) *and* Steamed Vegetables (bottom)

ALL–TIME FAVORITE BARBECUE SAUCE

1 can (10¾ ounces) CAMPBELL'S condensed Tomato Soup
¼ cup vinegar
¼ cup vegetable oil
2 tablespoons packed brown sugar
1 tablespoon Worcestershire sauce
1 teaspoon garlic powder
⅛ teaspoon Louisiana-style hot sauce (optional)

■ In small bowl, combine soup, vinegar, oil, brown sugar, Worcestershire sauce, garlic powder and hot sauce; set aside. Use sauce to baste ribs, chicken, hamburgers or steak during broiling or grilling.

Makes about 1⅓ cups sauce	Prep Time: 5 minutes

CHEDDAR CHEESE SAUCE

1 can (10¾ ounces) CAMPBELL'S condensed Cheddar Cheese Soup
⅓ cup milk
Paprika for garnish

■ In 1-quart saucepan, combine soup and milk. Over medium heat, heat through, stirring often. Serve over French fries, broccoli, cauliflower, carrots, baked potatoes or omelets. Sprinkle with paprika, if desired.

Makes about 1½ cups sauce	Prep Time: 5 minutes Cook Time: 5 minutes

Cheese Sauce Dijonnaise: Prepare Cheddar Cheese Sauce as directed above, *except* add 1 tablespoon *Dijon-style mustard* with the milk.

All-Time Favorite Barbecue Sauce (left) *and* **Cheddar Cheese Sauce (right)**

BROCCOLI–CHEESE POTATO TOPPER

1 can (10¾ ounces) CAMPBELL'S condensed Cream of Celery Soup
½ cup shredded Cheddar *or* Swiss cheese (2 ounces)
1 teaspoon Dijon-style mustard
⅛ teaspoon black pepper
2 cups cooked broccoli flowerets
4 hot baked potatoes, split lengthwise

■ In 2-quart saucepan, combine soup, Cheddar cheese, mustard and black pepper. Over low heat, heat until cheese is melted, stirring often. Add broccoli. Heat through, stirring occasionally. Serve over potatoes.

Makes about 2 cups sauce or 4 side-dish servings	Prep Time: 10 minutes Cook Time: 10 minutes

Tip For oven-baked potatoes, scrub 4 potatoes (8 ounces *each*); pierce each potato with fork several times. Bake at 400°F. for 1 hour or until fork-tender. (For micro-cooked potatoes, see directions on page 56.)

CHICKEN–BROCCOLI SAUCE

Pictured opposite, this extra-easy sauce is spooned over grilled chicken and served with Italian vinaigrette drizzled over thinly sliced cucumbers.

1 can (10¾ ounces) CAMPBELL'S condensed Cream of Chicken & Broccoli Soup
½ cup milk
⅛ teaspoon black pepper

■ In 1-quart saucepan, combine soup, milk and black pepper. Over medium heat, heat through, stirring often. Serve over broiled or grilled chicken, or hot cooked rice or noodles.

Makes about 1½ cups sauce	Prep Time: 5 minutes Cook Time: 5 minutes

Broccoli-Cheese Potato Topper (top) *and* Chicken-Broccoli Sauce (bottom)

Index

Recipes by Product